This journal belongs to:

_____

_____

_____

_____

Date:

Verse:

Thoughts & Notes:

Prayer Requests:

Date:

Verse:

Thoughts & Notes:

Prayer Requests:

Date:

Verse:

Thoughts & Notes:

Prayer Requests:

Date:

Verse:

Thoughts & Notes:

Prayer Requests:

Date:

Verse:

Thoughts & Notes:

Prayer Requests:

Date:

Verse:

Thoughts & Notes:

Prayer Requests:

Date:

Verse:

Thoughts & Notes:

Prayer Requests:

Date:

Verse:

Thoughts & Notes:

Prayer Requests:

Date:

Verse:

Thoughts & Notes:

Prayer Requests:

Date:

Verse:

Thoughts & Notes:

Prayer Requests:

Date:

Verse:

Thoughts & Notes:

Prayer Requests:

Date:

Verse:

Thoughts & Notes:

Prayer Requests:

Date:

Verse:

Thoughts & Notes:

Prayer Requests:

Date:

Verse:

Thoughts & Notes:

Prayer Requests:

Date:

Verse:

Thoughts & Notes:

Prayer Requests:

Date:

Verse:

Thoughts & Notes:

Prayer Requests:

Date:

Verse:

Thoughts & Notes:

Prayer Requests:

Date:

Verse:

Thoughts & Notes:

Prayer Requests:

Date:

Verse:

Thoughts & Notes:

Prayer Requests:

Date:

Verse:

Thoughts & Notes:

Prayer Requests:

Date:

Verse:

Thoughts & Notes:

Prayer Requests:

Date:

Verse:

Thoughts & Notes:

Prayer Requests:

Date:

Verse:

Thoughts & Notes:

Prayer Requests:

Date:

Verse:

Thoughts & Notes:

Prayer Requests:

Date:

Verse:

Thoughts & Notes:

Prayer Requests:

Date:

Verse:

Thoughts & Notes:

Prayer Requests:

Date:

Verse:

Thoughts & Notes:

Prayer Requests:

Date:

Verse:

Thoughts & Notes:

Prayer Requests:

Date:

Verse:

Thoughts & Notes:

Prayer Requests:

Date:

Verse:

Thoughts & Notes:

Prayer Requests:

Date:

Verse:

Thoughts & Notes:

Prayer Requests:

Date:

Verse:

Thoughts & Notes:

Prayer Requests:

Date:

Verse:

Thoughts & Notes:

Prayer Requests:

Date:

Verse:

Thoughts & Notes:

Prayer Requests:

Date:

Verse:

Thoughts & Notes:

Prayer Requests:

Date:

Verse:

Thoughts & Notes:

Prayer Requests:

Date:

Verse:

Thoughts & Notes:

Prayer Requests:

Date:

Verse:

Thoughts & Notes:

Prayer Requests:

Date:

Verse:

Thoughts & Notes:

Prayer Requests:

Date:

Verse:

Thoughts & Notes:

Prayer Requests:

Date:

Verse:

Thoughts & Notes:

Prayer Requests:

Date:

Verse:

Thoughts & Notes:

Prayer Requests:

Date:

Verse:

Thoughts & Notes:

Prayer Requests:

Date:

Verse:

Thoughts & Notes:

Prayer Requests:

Date:

Verse:

Thoughts & Notes:

Prayer Requests:

Date:

Verse:

Thoughts & Notes:

Prayer Requests:

Date:

Verse:

Thoughts & Notes:

Prayer Requests:

Date:

Verse:

Thoughts & Notes:

Prayer Requests:

Date:

Verse:

Thoughts & Notes:

Prayer Requests:

Date:

Verse:

Thoughts & Notes:

Prayer Requests:

Date:

Verse:

Thoughts & Notes:

Prayer Requests:

Date:

Verse:

Thoughts & Notes:

Prayer Requests:

Date:

Verse:

Thoughts & Notes:

Prayer Requests:

Date:

Verse:

Thoughts & Notes:

Prayer Requests:

Date:

Verse:

Thoughts & Notes:

Prayer Requests:

Date:

Verse:

Thoughts & Notes:

Prayer Requests:

Date:

Verse:

Thoughts & Notes:

Prayer Requests:

Date:

Verse:

Thoughts & Notes:

Prayer Requests:

Date:

Verse:

Thoughts & Notes:

Prayer Requests:

Date:

Verse:

Thoughts & Notes:

Prayer Requests:

Date:

Verse:

Thoughts & Notes:

Prayer Requests:

Date:

Verse:

Thoughts & Notes:

Prayer Requests:

Date:

Verse:

Thoughts & Notes:

Prayer Requests:

Date:

Verse:

Thoughts & Notes:

Prayer Requests:

Date:

Verse:

Thoughts & Notes:

Prayer Requests:

Date:

Verse:

Thoughts & Notes:

Prayer Requests:

Date:

Verse:

Thoughts & Notes:

Prayer Requests:

Date:

Verse:

Thoughts & Notes:

Prayer Requests:

Date:

Verse:

Thoughts & Notes:

Prayer Requests:

Date:

Verse:

Thoughts & Notes:

Prayer Requests:

Date:

Verse:

Thoughts & Notes:

Prayer Requests:

Date:

Verse:

Thoughts & Notes:

Prayer Requests:

Date:

Verse:

Thoughts & Notes:

Prayer Requests:

Date:

Verse:

Thoughts & Notes:

Prayer Requests:

Date:

Verse:

Thoughts & Notes:

Prayer Requests:

Date:

Verse:

Thoughts & Notes:

Prayer Requests:

Date:

Verse:

Thoughts & Notes:

Prayer Requests:

Date:

Verse:

Thoughts & Notes:

Prayer Requests:

Date:

Verse:

Thoughts & Notes:

Prayer Requests:

Date:

Verse:

Thoughts & Notes:

Prayer Requests:

Date:

Verse:

Thoughts & Notes:

Prayer Requests:

Date:

Verse:

Thoughts & Notes:

Prayer Requests:

Date:

Verse:

Thoughts & Notes:

Prayer Requests:

Date:

Verse:

Thoughts & Notes:

Prayer Requests:

Date:

Verse:

Thoughts & Notes:

Prayer Requests:

Date:

Verse:

Thoughts & Notes:

Prayer Requests:

Date:

Verse:

Thoughts & Notes:

Prayer Requests:

Date:

Verse:

Thoughts & Notes:

Prayer Requests:

Date:

Verse:

Thoughts & Notes:

Prayer Requests:

Date:

Verse:

Thoughts & Notes:

Prayer Requests:

Date:

Verse:

Thoughts & Notes:

Prayer Requests:

Date:

Verse:

Thoughts & Notes:

Prayer Requests:

Date:

Verse:

Thoughts & Notes:

Prayer Requests:

Date:

Verse:

Thoughts & Notes:

Prayer Requests:

Date:

Verse:

Thoughts & Notes:

Prayer Requests:

Date:

Verse:

Thoughts & Notes:

Prayer Requests:

Date:

Verse:

Thoughts & Notes:

Prayer Requests:

Date:

Verse:

Thoughts & Notes:

Prayer Requests:

Date:

Verse:

Thoughts & Notes:

Prayer Requests:

Date:

Verse:

Thoughts & Notes:

Prayer Requests:

Date:

Verse:

Thoughts & Notes:

Prayer Requests:

Date:

Verse:

Thoughts & Notes:

Prayer Requests:

Date:

Verse:

Thoughts & Notes:

Prayer Requests:

Date:

Verse:

Thoughts & Notes:

Prayer Requests:

Date:

Verse:

Thoughts & Notes:

Prayer Requests:

Date:

Verse:

Thoughts & Notes:

Prayer Requests:

Date:

Verse:

Thoughts & Notes:

Prayer Requests:

Date:

Verse:

Thoughts & Notes:

Prayer Requests:

Date:

Verse:

Thoughts & Notes:

Prayer Requests:

Date:

Verse:

Thoughts & Notes:

Prayer Requests:

Date:

Verse:

Thoughts & Notes:

Prayer Requests:

Date:

Verse:

Thoughts & Notes:

Prayer Requests:

Date:

Verse:

Thoughts & Notes:

Prayer Requests:

Date:

Verse:

Thoughts & Notes:

Prayer Requests:

Date:

Verse:

Thoughts & Notes:

Prayer Requests:

Date:

Verse:

Thoughts & Notes:

Prayer Requests:

Date:

Verse:

Thoughts & Notes:

Prayer Requests:

Date:

Verse:

Thoughts & Notes:

Prayer Requests:

Date:

Verse:

Thoughts & Notes:

Prayer Requests:

Date:

Verse:

Thoughts & Notes:

Prayer Requests:

Date:

Verse:

Thoughts & Notes:

Prayer Requests:

Date:

Verse:

Thoughts & Notes:

Prayer Requests:

Date:

Verse:

Thoughts & Notes:

Prayer Requests:

Date:

Verse:

Thoughts & Notes:

Prayer Requests:

Date:

Verse:

Thoughts & Notes:

Prayer Requests:

Date:

Verse:

Thoughts & Notes:

Prayer Requests:

Date:

Verse:

Thoughts & Notes:

Prayer Requests:

Date:

Verse:

Thoughts & Notes:

Prayer Requests:

Date:

Verse:

Thoughts & Notes:

Prayer Requests:

Date:

Verse:

Thoughts & Notes:

Prayer Requests:

Date:

Verse:

Thoughts & Notes:

Prayer Requests:

Date:

Verse:

Thoughts & Notes:

Prayer Requests:

Date:

Verse:

Thoughts & Notes:

Prayer Requests:

Date:

Verse:

Thoughts & Notes:

Prayer Requests:

Date:

Verse:

Thoughts & Notes:

Prayer Requests:

Date:

Verse:

Thoughts & Notes:

Prayer Requests:

Date:

Verse:

Thoughts & Notes:

Prayer Requests:

Date:

Verse:

Thoughts & Notes:

Prayer Requests:

Date:

Verse:

Thoughts & Notes:

Prayer Requests:

Date:

Verse:

Thoughts & Notes:

Prayer Requests:

Date:

Verse:

Thoughts & Notes:

Prayer Requests:

Date:

Verse:

Thoughts & Notes:

Prayer Requests:

Date:

Verse:

Thoughts & Notes:

Prayer Requests:

Date:

Verse:

Thoughts & Notes:

Prayer Requests:

Date:

Verse:

Thoughts & Notes:

Prayer Requests:

Date:

Verse:

Thoughts & Notes:

Prayer Requests:

Date:

Verse:

Thoughts & Notes:

Prayer Requests:

Date:

Verse:

Thoughts & Notes:

Prayer Requests:

Date:

Verse:

Thoughts & Notes:

Prayer Requests:

Made in the USA
Monee, IL
27 February 2025

13019254R00083